A BRIDGE

Exploring the Connections Between
A Course in Miracles

A Course of Love

By Friends of Both Courses

This work is dedicated to those students of A Course in Miracles who are open to discover whether another gift is now available to them.

Most direct quotations from both *A Course in Miracles* and *A Course of Love* are in italics. The referencing system to text within ACOL, briefly, follows this pattern: **Book:Chapter.Paragraph**

"The Course," or Book One, is referenced as C.

"The Treatises," or Book Two, is referenced as T1, T2, T3, or T4 (there are four Treatises)

"The Dialogues," or Book Three, is referenced as D.

Thus, C:20.30 refers to The Course, ch. 20, para. 30

References to The Forty Days and Forty Nights are, for example, D:Day1.23

References within the Introduction, the Prelude, the Epilogue, or the Addendum are simply to the paragraph number therein, for example, I.13, P.8, E.20, or A.14

Book design and computer production by Patty Arnold, *Menagerie Design & Publishing*

TAKE HEART PUBLICATIONS
A nonprofit publisher
12402 Bitney Springs Road
Nevada City, CA 95959
www.takeheartpublications.org
530-274-7797
info@takeheartpublications.org

Printed in the United States of America
ISBN 978-1-58469-665-0

It is difficult to understand what "The Kingdom of Heaven is within you" means. The reason is because it is not understandable to the ego, which interprets it as if something outside is inside, which does not mean anything.

The word "within" does not belong. The Kingdom of Heaven **is** you. What else but you did the Creator create, and what else **but** you **is** His Kingdom? This is the whole message of the Atonement, a message which in its totality transcends the sum of the parts . . .

(ACIM, COA ed., T-4.V.1, emphasis in original)

Table of Contents

The Main Contributors 7

Introduction *10*

An Overview of ACOL and How It Relates to ACIM . . . *12*

   1. Why *A Course of Love*? 12

   2. Why would there be "*A Course of Love*" if love
      cannot be taught? 13

   3. What is the purpose of ACOL and how does it relate to the
      purpose of ACIM? 15

   4. How does ACOL compare to ACIM? 15

   5. Please elaborate on how the two Courses compare. 16

   6. Both ACIM and ACOL mention attainment of a
      "happy dream." Sounds nice. Is that the goal? 18

Is the World (and the Body) Real? *20*

   7. What is the fundamental outlook of both ACIM and
      ACOL on the world? 20

   8. ACIM famously says that the world is an illusion.
      ACOL says that all of creation, including the world,
      is made in God's own image. Please explain. 21

   9. ACIM is clear about everything temporal being illusory.
      In what sense could I ever be brought to understand that
      form is divine? 23

  10. But I have been told that according to ACIM, the world
      itself is illusory. Have I misunderstood ACIM? Is ACOL
      saying something different? 25

11. ACIM says that the body is an illusion, a miscreation based in fear. ACOL says that the choice to experience a body is simply a choice, a choice that is "consistent with the laws of love." Why this shift? 26

12. ACIM says that truth cannot be brought to illusion; rather, illusion must be brought to truth for correction. ACOL's concept of an "elevated Self of form" seems like an attempt to bring truth to illusion. Can you explain? 28

The Role of Mind, Heart, Feeling, and Relationship . . . 31

13. ACOL puts a huge emphasis on "wholeheartedness." What is meant by that? 31

14. Does ACOL denigrate the mind? 35

15. ACIM says that pain is the result of guilt, whereas ACOL says that pain is the result of feelings of lack of love. Why the difference?. 36

16. I have the impression that ACOL deals a lot with feelings and emotions. Is this true? 36

   ✖ Let's start with negative feelings.. 36

   ✖ And yet, ACOL says there are no "bad" feelings. What are we to do with our feelings? 37

   ✖ Feelings are a doorway to God. 38

17. When reading ACOL, there is such an emphasis on "relationship" – not only to other people but to everything. Why is relationship such a big deal? 40

18. Does ACOL treat gender issues differently from ACIM? . . . 42

Learning vs. Knowing, and the End of Learning. 42

19. ACOL tells us that "the time of learning" is over. What does this mean? 42

20. ACIM speaks of how entrenched the ego is. ACOL tells the reader that "the ego-self is gone." Why this big shift? . . . 44

21: ACOL asks us to "learn in a new way." Is it really new? . . . 45

22. ACOL holds out the possibility of "direct learning."
How does this happen? 48

23. ACOL tells us that "the time of the Holy Spirit" is over.
Please explain.. 49

24. Many people have set themselves up as ACIM teachers.
ACOL seems almost "beyond teaching." Is this true?. 50

Significant and Distinctive Terms Used in ACOL 52

25. ACOL speaks a lot of "the New." What is meant by the New? . 52

26. ACOL seems to celebrate us as being "The Accomplished,"
with the ego now gone. Sounds too good to be true! 54

27. ACOL repeatedly says that "giving and receiving are one."
Please explain.. 57

28. Our "separation" from God is the source of our problem.
Yet ACOL says we are "differentiated," and that this
is necessary. What is the difference between being
separate and being differentiated? 58

29. ACOL speaks of the fulfillment of the Way of Jesus, and then
introduces the Way of Mary. What does this mean?. 60

30. I have heard that ACOL concludes with a "Forty Days
and Forty Nights" section in the final book. Can you
summarize the content of that section? 62

Resources 63

The Main Contributors

The idea for this booklet germinated at a Course in Miracles conference when it was felt that *A Course of Love* (ACOL) was being misunderstood and therefore misrepresented by some. Over the space of a year, the following contributors assembled a few topics and a few clarifications that they felt merit particular attention. The contributor of each "answer" is identified, in part to emphasize that there are no "right" or "wrong" answers, in keeping with ACOL's approach to truth—that *the only correct interpretation is that which comes from each reader's own internal guidance system.* (A.15) The perspectives shared are their own and do not necessarily represent those of Mari Perron, the First Receiver of ACOL, or the publisher.

SUSAN BERNARDINI:

I have always been a spiritual seeker. At five I wondered, "Why is there a "here?" After my father died unexpectedly in 1994, I had a reoccurring dream about a blue book on a shelf in the local bookstore. I found the book exactly where it was in my dream. It was *A Course in Miracles.* I was a student and teacher of ACIM for almost 20 years when I discovered an online advertisement that said there was a "new course in Miracles." I was skeptical but intrigued, so I bought an electronic version. Before I read the first sentence, I thought, "Nothing will EVER replace ACIM in my heart, soul, and life."

I hadn't finished chapter 1 of ACOL before I knew this was the voice I had come to love and trust. Jesus seemed to be speaking directly to me in a deeply personal way. I felt known and cherished, and in acceptance of myself, others, and life. ACOL has not diminished my love of ACIM. It has increased it. ACIM has taken on a new clarity and simplicity since studying ACOL. I have stopped seeking. With ACOL, I feel like I have found the way home.

LAUREL ELSTROM:

I was born spiritually hungry. In my large family, I have always been the devoted one. My quest for truth began in the Pentecostal church where I was raised. Over the years, I explored many other religions, philosophies, and teachings, and have found truth at the core of them all. Twenty-five years ago, *A Course in Miracles* brought me exciting and transformative revelations, unraveling many layers of lies. Still, I longed for more. Five years ago, *A Course of Love* chose me and has gloriously carried me to an ongoing dance with freedom. ACOL is not the only path to awakening, but it is a powerful gift for ACIM students and others who long to awaken while still embodied. It can be difficult for those who love and trust ACIM to accept any other written work. Yet I have witnessed with my own eyes the transformative power of ACOL. For many, it is the next step.

My experience with ACOL came with a clear and definitive calling to write and teach. The Voice that guides me is crystal clear: provide resources and support for ACOL students. In response, I recorded one hundred and eight videos summarizing each chapter of ACOL on my youtube channel. I frequently contribute to "The Embrace," the ACOL monthly newsletter, and was recently published in Great Britain's "Miracle Worker" magazine. A three-year labor of love, *Love on the Mountain: An Inquiry Companion to the Forty Days and Forty Nights of A Course of Love* will be published in 2019.

I continue to lead a long-term ACOL study group in Asheville, North Carolina and am a certified professional coach specializing in one-on-one sessions with ACOL students. I can be reached at laurelelstrom@gmail.com and through my website, www.laurelelstrom.com.

GLENN HOVEMANN:

For almost the full decade of the '70s I lived in a community that I had co-founded in Oregon. One day an unknown visitor approached me. "I think these are for you," she said, as she handed me three big blue hardcover books. The year was 1978. When I looked into those books I *knew* they spoke truth—and I knew that I didn't understand them. Thus began many years of deepening into ACIM. Over the decades I still explored with many other teachers, but Jesus was bedrock, and ACIM was his powerful message. Yet still I felt, somehow, that there was more to be revealed.

In early 2013 I discovered ACOL, self-published by Mari Perron in three volumes. It was like coming home, revelatory and transformative. Later that year Mari asked me, to my surprise, to publish ACOL. (My wife, Muffy, and I were publishers—of children's picture books, mostly!) I hesitated, but the call was clear. In early 2014 Mari confirmed her request and Muffy and I formed Take Heart Publications to publish and promote ACOL in English and to oversee foreign translations.

MICHAEL MARK:

I was raised a Catholic, but was also very curious about other spiritual traditions, both Eastern and Western. I once attended a talk given by a Native American elder, where I was struck by this person's obvious connection to a living reality. It was humbling, and released a desire deep within me to be on similar terms with my Creator.

I tried to move in the direction of my desires, but before long I was depressed and uncertain of myself. There was a gap between who I was in the world, and who I felt I could be in reality, that I couldn't cross. My mind was thus well-prepared to discover *A Course in Miracles*.

I devoted myself to the study of ACIM for about fifteen years, and completed the entire workbook of exercises two times through. I found myself able to choose peace on a consistent basis, and then began to feel there was something more. A joy was welling up inside me that wasn't for me alone, and I wasn't sure what to do with it. My heart was thus well-prepared to discover *A Course of Love*.

There is indeed something more than being at peace: there is being in Love. ACOL guided me to the knowledge that we can only experience the reality of who we are through Creation—through experiencing what lies beyond conceptual understanding. For this, and for the opportunity to share here, I am grateful.

Introduction

Although the three books that comprise *A Course of Love* had been previously published, it was not until the work's more formal publication in 2014 by Take Heart Publications that the Course in Miracles community began to take significant notice of this work. The response since then has been mixed, which is not unexpected, but one element of the response that has been concerning to the authors of this booklet is the depiction of ACOL by some leaders of the ACIM community as being contradictory to the core teachings of ACIM. At various times, ACOL has been described as a regression, as a likely cause of confusion to ACIM students, and as a more "comforting" spiritual teaching for those individuals who, for whatever reason, may be unwilling to undertake the "real" work prescribed by ACIM.

The purpose of this document is to offer another perspective on the relationship between ACIM and ACOL for those who may seek it. For the contributors to this volume, who have benefited greatly from both Courses, it can be difficult to understand why our love of ACOL and the enhancement that it has brought to our understanding of ACIM makes our paths "regressions" from the path offered by ACIM.

There are only a couple of reasons that anyone would make statements to the world at large about the priority of one spiritual teaching with regard to another. One stems from the desire to help our fellow human beings by sharing something we have learned that we feel is truly helpful. The second is to defend a set of cherished ideas from perceived dilution, abrogation, or misinterpretation. In either case, there are some very fine lines here that may be crossed, even with the best of intentions.

The idea that any of us may know what is best for another is one of those pitfalls, and it stems from the notion that a particular conceptual orientation has the power to end the tragedy of our seeming separation. The ability to recite the Koran, or quote the Bible, or offer a line from our favorite Course means precious little. We are not after intellectual understanding with these Courses, but freedom from the illusion that we are separate from God. This freedom is a return to the fullness and sanctity of our own heart, our One Heart, where our relationship to God begins and ends. Meanwhile, it matters not what words we adopt as our own, for until we discover the Word itself, which God has written upon our hearts, all the other words are simply constructs. Without the miracle, which none of us control, all such words are empty.

Each of us knows from past experience that we once fell prey to a misperception—one so complete and so profound that we were helpless to awaken from it. But for the miracle, every one of us would truly be lost. It is natural when awakening from this dream to wish to share our relief with others, but a mind that does not see as many miracles waiting in the wings as there are beings in need of receiving them, is still misperceiving, just as a mind that sees others as lost without its name brand of help is mistaken. The assertion that an "other" is not capable of discerning the truth in the quiet of his or her own heart is only giving a sound basis for fear. For how can what really matters—genuine knowledge of the Kingdom that we already are—be restored if what lies within cannot be trusted? None of us know the path another will take to freedom. None of us know the words, or moments, or miraculous encounters that will lead home.

The contributors to this work are unanimously of the opinion that ACOL and ACIM have been of tremendous value to their healing paths. The vantages we offer herein are our own, given in an effort to share a perspective—not to insist it is the only possible experience of these two works, or the only proper understanding of them.

This work is presented as a series of questions and answers, and the author of each response to each question has been indicated. Our intent is to avoid the suggestion there is any one form of answering these questions that is exclusively correct, and to avoid the solidification of answers into dogmas or ideals. Some of our contributors are more verbose than others. Some have different vantages. We view this as all of a piece, as we are each unique expressions of the fullness of God. Words remain but symbols. The truth is what lives and breathes and dances in our own hearts. It is the living reality of Love we would remember, and to which we would each return.

Above all we hope that this little booklet is truly helpful to you.

An Overview of ACOL and How It Relates to ACIM

1. Why A Course of Love?

GLENN:

The urgency of the need for humankind to truly recognize unity is, Jesus stated, *the only reason for this continuation of the coursework provided in A Course in Miracles.* (A.4)

In the decades that have passed since Helen Schucman heard the inner voice and scribed ACIM, many related works have been written. And yet no other inner voice heard as Jesus proclaimed that it was another "Course." The first words Mari Perron "heard" in 1998—the words that begin the Prelude—were, *This is a course in miracles.*

At the end of the Prelude Jesus named his new Course: *This time we take a direct approach, an approach that seems at first to leave behind abstract learning and the complex mechanisms of the mind that so betray you. We take a step away from intellect, the pride of the ego, and approach this final learning through the realm of the heart. This is why, to end confusion, we call this course A Course of Love.*

Each Course was received in a similar manner from a source that identified itself as Jesus. In both Courses, Jesus does not cloak his identity. Sometimes he refers to himself explicitly, sometimes contextually; usually in the first person, sometimes in the third person. ACIM focuses especially on preparing the mind; ACOL, the heart. Both are needed.

MICHAEL:

Because I believe that ACOL is a close relation to ACIM, it is natural for me to begin there, and ask, "Why a Course in Miracles?"

ACIM is clear on its objective. *The goal of the curriculum, regardless of the teacher you choose, is 'Know thyself.' There is nothing else to seek. Everyone is looking for himself and for the power and glory he thinks he has lost.* (T-8.III.5:1-3) This goal, as well as the need for a shift in perception that will precede knowledge itself, is consistently expressed in ACOL, which says, *The loftiest aim of which you are currently capable is that of changing your perception. Although our ultimate goal is to move beyond perception to knowledge, a first step in doing this is changing your means of perception to that of right-mindedness.* (C:19.23)

In an ultimate sense, the "why" of the two Courses is identical, but there is a question contained within this question that has not been answered yet, and it is this: Why, unless something has gone wrong, or ACIM itself was incomplete, would another Course be necessary? Didn't ACIM give us all that is required for the dissolution of the ego and our return to Love's embrace? It may seem to some students of ACIM that the emergence of a second Course belies a shortcoming of the first, but I don't believe this is the case at all. The existence of ACOL implies neither a flaw in ACIM, nor a requirement that to obtain a "complete" understanding one must also read ACOL.

The answer to the question that has not been asked is that we have not fully learned all that ACIM offered to us, and in response to the direction we have taken the teachings of ACIM, a response in turn has been given.

ACOL offers this sentiment directly: *Until you have truly recognized unity . . . you continue to perceive of yourself as a learning being. This is the only reason for this continuation of the coursework provided in A Course in Miracles. While you continue to put effort into learning what cannot be learned, as you continue to see yourself as a student seeking to acquire what you do not yet have, you cannot recognize the unity in which you exist and be freed from learning forever.* (A.4)

The "why" of a Course of Love, while being virtually identical to the "why" of A Course in Miracles, is simple: We are loved, and the assistance will continue until we have fully remembered and accepted the truth of who we are.

2. Why would there be "A Course of Love" if love cannot be taught?

GLENN:

ACIM says that it *does not aim at teaching the meaning of love, for that is beyond what can be taught. It does aim, however, at removing the blocks to the awareness of love's presence, which is your natural inheritance.* (Tx.I.2)

ACOL explains why love itself is beyond the curriculum: *Love has no attributes, which is why it cannot be taught.* (C:2.4)

So how does Jesus propose to reveal love through his Course of Love? In the same way as in ACIM, by removing the blocks to the awareness of love's presence: *Remember that your task here is to remove the barriers that keep you from realizing what love is. That is the learning goal of this Course—your awareness of what love is—and no earthly course can take you beyond this goal. It is only your willingness that is required.* (C:11.5) That is, a willingness to release fear. *Because you have not properly recognized fear as nothing, you have not properly recognized love as everything.* (C:2.4)

Which brings us back to the matter of attributes: *It is because of the attributes you have given fear that love has been given attributes. Only separate things have attributes . . .* (C:2.4) In other words, the mistake we made was identifying Love as being the attributes we assigned it. Thus we could love hot chocolate without making the mistake of thinking that love IS hot chocolate.

How does Jesus go about removing our barriers to our true Self, which is love? Through relationships. This can be no surprise, given the extraordinary emphasis on relationships in both Courses. *To think of achieving love "on one's own" is ludicrous.* (C:1.12) This is not a matter of entering nice or even loving "relationships" as we usually understand them, but for true forgiveness and "joining." Joining with Jesus, with God, and with all beings—especially the Christ "part" of us. *Reality, the truly real, is relationship.* (C:6.1) True joining and relationship, he says, entails a mutual "ownership," no longer two but one, in which we are each one another's "own," and that we are each God's "own," for what God has joined can never truly be separate. *It means a love deeper than any love you have known, for in not owning and possessing, in not being owned and possessed by, and in, union and relationship, you have not fully known love.* (D:Day38.10)

3. What is the purpose of ACOL and how does it relate to the purpose of ACIM?

GLENN:

Jesus is very clear about the purpose, and the success, of ACIM: *The world as a state of being, as a whole, has entered a time, brought on largely by A Course in Miracles, in which readiness for miracle-mindedness is upon it. A Course in Miracles opened a door by threatening the ego. All those who, with egos weakened, walked this world with the hope of leaving ego behind, with miracle-minded intent, have awakened human beings to a new identity. They have ushered in a time of ending our identity crisis. Not since Jesus walked the earth has such a time been upon humankind.* (C:P.5)

The relationship between the Courses, he says, is a very close one: *A Course in Miracles and A Course of Love work hand-in-hand because the change of thinking taught within A Course in Miracles was a change of thinking about yourself. It attempted to dislodge the ego-mind that has provided you with an identity that you but think you are. A Course of Love then followed in order to reveal to you who you truly are.* (T2:4.3)

The revelation of "who we truly are" is the goal we seek, often in the guise of something else (such as God or enlightenment). Even the mere idea of knowing who we truly are, knowing ourselves at last, can bring unexpected tears of hope and relief.

4. How does ACOL compare to ACIM?

BY GUEST CONTRIBUTOR REV. TONY PONTICELLO OF THE COMMUNITY MIRACLES CENTER

People ask me this a lot. How I am guided to answer this question at this moment is that I do NOT think the teachings themselves are radically different. What I think ACOL "corrects" is not the teaching of ACIM. It corrects the direction that the discussion and practice of ACIM has veered off into. For years now an over intellectual, didactic, psychological approach seems to have taken hold of the ACIM Community. ACOL is a "mid-course" correction back into a more loving, expansive, and truly miraculous direction. I am most excited about ACOL's emphasis on the end of traditional learning and the ready embrace of an experience of life that is entirely new.

5. Please elaborate on how the two Courses compare.

MICHAEL:

As the first of the two Courses received, ACIM is for minds unable to distinguish the false from the true. Believing in the validity of their own projections, such minds are snared in a state of conflict which they cannot, of their own devices, unravel. Ultimately, they experience themselves as separate from their Creator, and from Love itself. This belief is evidenced most clearly in the idea that we are bodies—bodies separable from one another, bodies that can win while others lose, bodies that can break down and die, bodies that can take from other bodies—bodies that make the ideas of loss, vulnerability, and suffering eminently tangible.

The remedy for this offered in ACIM is the correction of errors through the practice of the thought system described. ACIM is clear from the outset that it *is a course in mind training.* (T-1.VII.4) This idea is echoed in the Manual for Teachers, which states, *It cannot be too strongly emphasized that this course aims at a complete reversal of thought.* (M-24.4) Some goals of this training are *to teach you that the ego is unbelievable and will forever be unbelievable,* (T-7.VIII-7) to enable *the escape from fear,* (T-9.II.1), *to teach what is the same and what is different* (T-26.III.5) and *to teach that all miracles are the same.* (T-26.V.1)

The core ideas of ACIM all relate to the correction of past learning errors, and the primary teaching method offered is one of contrast. The body is contrasted with the spirit, time with eternity, guilt with innocence, conflict with peace, God's will with the ego's will, the truth with the false, and reality with illusion. As we withdraw our investment from ego's the thought system and accept the thought system of the Holy Spirit, the conditions produced by our conflicted, fearful thoughts fall away, and only what is real remains.

ACOL was received approximately thirty years after ACIM, and the text itself provides a clear statement of its relationship to ACIM. *Where the original Course in Miracles was a course in thought reversal and mind training, a course to point out the insanity of the identity crisis and dislodge the ego's hold, this is a course to establish your identity and end the reign of the ego.* (C:P.8)

The approaches of the two Courses are very different: where ACIM was written primarily for minds caught in the crises of their own misperceptions, ACOL was written primarily for the heart. The heart is the part of the mind that has never forgotten God. ACIM says in the Workbook, *There is an ancient peace you carry in your heart and have not lost.* (W-164.4) Thus, while ACIM seeks to dismantle the ego's insane thought system, ACOL seeks to awaken the remembrance of truth within us by speaking directly to the heart.

The emphasis in ACOL is upon reunifying the heart and mind to restore the condition described as "wholeheartedness," which can only occur when the mind accepts the thought system of the truth and releases the power of the heart. With this *first joining*, the time of learning comes to an end and we accept the mantle of our true identity in Christ—an identity we share.

The emphasis in ACOL is upon the completion of learning and the acceptance of our true identity in Christ, for learning is only necessary while conflict and separation remain. Learning is described as *a pattern of divine design, created in unity and cooperation to enable the return to unity.* (D:2.4) The pathway given to the completion of learning is <u>acceptance</u>—acceptance of our divinity, of our true identity in Christ, and of our perfect accomplishment in the Mind of God. There is nothing we can do to become "better" versions of ourselves, and nothing we can do to atone for who we imagined we've been than to accept the Atonement given us. We are complete as God created us, and forever unchanging.

What occurs with the establishment of our true identity and a return to wholeheartedness is the restoration of our creative potential. The conflict, lack, and powerlessness we see in the world today is what we have made of this world, and is illusory in the sense that it need not be, and isn't everlasting—but while it remains in our experience we suffer needlessly. The key to transforming our world and birthing the divine pattern of creation is the acceptance of who we are. This is nothing short of the complete thought reversal first described in ACIM, given life and expression through the acceptance of our shared identity in Christ described in ACOL.

There are many linking themes between the two works—too many to describe herein—and many interesting parallels. Grievances as described in ACIM are paralleled by bitterness of the heart in ACOL. The rightmindedness of ACIM is paralleled with the wholehearted-ness of ACOL. Themes that resound in both courses include unity, holy relationship, forgiveness, abundance, miracles, revelation, and power. There are also ways in which ACOL extends the core ideas of ACIM into notions such as the creation of the new and life everlasting, which describe visions of a world transformed.

Addressing the full scope of ACIM and ACOL in this little booklet is impossible and probably not desirable. There are ideas in ACOL that have been described as being inconsistent with prevalent interpreta-tions of ACIM, and these will be discussed briefly herein. These are nuanced points of discussion which need not detract from the core message of both Courses: the correction of error, which we call the miracle, leads to the new life in Christ we've already been given.

6. Both ACIM and ACOL mention attainment of a "happy dream." Sounds nice. Is that the goal?

MICHAEL:

The attainment of happy dreams is not the stated goal of either Course.

ACIM is clear on its objective. *The goal of the curriculum, regard-less of the teacher you choose, is 'Know thyself.' There is nothing else to seek. Everyone is looking for himself and for the power and glory he thinks he has lost.* (T-8.III.5:1-3) This goal, as well as the need for a shift in perception that will precede knowledge itself, is consis-tently expressed in ACOL, which says, *The loftiest aim of which you are currently capable is that of changing your perception. Although our ultimate goal is to move beyond perception to knowledge, a first step in doing this is changing your means of perception to that of right-mindedness.* (C:19.23)

In ACIM the concept of happy dreams is used to describe a condition in which the learning mind has yet to awaken to complete knowledge, but has begun, in time, to believe in the voice of the Holy Spirit, and thus to perceive a world of peace and love, rather than one of conflict and hatred. This is a temporary state, but an important one because it is a condition in which the Mind is perceiving in accordance with the guidance of the Holy Spirit, and also because this condition leads to knowledge, which is the true goal of both Courses.

ACIM says of happy dreams, *You will first dream of peace, and then awaken to it. Your first exchange of what you made for what you want is the exchange of nightmares for the happy dreams of love. In these lie your true perceptions, for the Holy Spirit corrects the world of dreams, where all perception is. Knowledge needs no correction. Yet the dreams of love lead unto knowledge.* (T-13.VII.9:1-5)

ACOL mentions happy dreams only rarely. One instance occurs in a chapter entitled *The Embrace*, which contains a beautiful invitation from Jesus to embrace him, and the Love of all Creation. Jesus says, *This is a call to move now into my embrace and let yourself be comforted. Let the tears fall and the weight of your shoulders rest upon mine. Let me cradle your head against my breast as I stroke your hair and assure you that it will be all right. Realize that this is the whole world, the universe, the all of all in whose embrace you literally exist. Feel the gentleness and the love. Drink in the safety and the rest. Close your eyes and begin to see with an imagination that is beyond thought and words.* (ACOL C:20.2)

Later in this chapter Jesus says, *From here your life becomes imaginal, a dream that requires you not to leave your home, your place of safety and of rest. You are cradled gently while your spirit soars, dreaming <u>happy dreams</u> at last. With love surrounding you in arms that hold you close, you feel the heartbeat of the world just beneath your resting head. It thunders in your ears and moves through* *you until there is no distinction. We are the heartbeat of the world.* (emphasis added)

This is creation. This is God. This is our home. (ACOL C:20.10-11)

It is clear to me that Jesus is speaking from his heart to ours, inviting us into the experience of Love. This passage gives a beautiful example of the way ACOL calls to our hearts, for no analysis of what a happy dream is or isn't is required to accept this invitation. We don't need to concern ourselves with the possibility that we might be happy, but still dreaming. We don't need to understand if we're "there yet" or not. Such notions are meaningless, and merely dissolve with our acceptance of Oneness.

In this same passage, Jesus says, *Within the embrace our sight clears and what we see is known rather than understood.* (C:20.8) Here Jesus is clear: salvation does not rest on conceptual understanding, but on the complete acceptance of the Love that we are. This Love can only be known, not understood, which is why it cannot be taught.

This question about happy dreams is difficult for me to answer conceptually, because at some level it just doesn't matter. To evaluate the two Courses on how they use these terms is, in my opinion, a form of hair-splitting that serves scholarship at the expense of direct contact with Love itself. Jesus has invited us to remember the One Heart we share. We need only say yes.

Is the World (and the Body) Real?

7. What is the fundamental outlook of both ACIM and ACOL on the world?

LAUREL:

The fundamental outlooks of both courses depend on how we see ourselves. Our worlds are a reflection and interpretation of what we believe. ACIM and ACOL both teach that a separated world isn't accurate. ACIM teaches the falseness of separation by exposing the smallness and cruelty of an ego-driven world. When we believe we are separated, vulnerable beings, self-defense is our only means of survival. As separated beings, we are compelled to be vicious, selfish, and reliant on complex defense mechanisms. There are no other means for an ego to survive. An ego that is believed into existence is frail and easily broken. The ego's house of cards is built on a fragile frame of the fundamental lie of separation. A world founded on a lie can never satisfy.

When the ego's falseness is exposed, as it is in ACIM, where does that leave us? ACIM tells us, "In my defenselessness, my safety lies." Why does defenseless make us safe? Because an ego cannot survive without defenses.

When the ego is exposed and abandoned, what remains? If we are not egos, who are we? This is the fundamental question of ACOL. The primary objective of ACOL is to guide readers toward firsthand discovery of who we actually are. Once the Self is known, and intimacy with life is re-established, interaction in the world becomes a responsive and cooperative dance.

ACIM exposes the false self and un-does much of the programming that sustains the ego. ACOL encourages discovery of the One Self with an invitation for a unique and differentiated experience from within the wholeness of the One energy, which is love.

8. **ACIM famously says that the world is an illusion. ACOL says that all of creation, including the world, is made in God's own image. Please explain.**

MICHAEL:

ACIM does say, in Lesson 155, that the world is an illusion. Let us look at this statement in the context of the two paragraphs that bracket it. (The underlined passages are referenced below.)

There is a way of living in the world that is not here, although it seems to be. You do not change appearance, though you smile more frequently. Your forehead is serene; your eyes are quiet. And the ones who walk the world as you do recognize their own. Yet those who have not yet perceived the way will recognize you also, and believe that you are like them, as you were before.

The world is an illusion. Those who choose to come to it are seeking for a place where they can be illusions, and avoid their own reality. Yet when they find their own reality is even here, then they step back and let it lead the way. What other choice is really theirs to make? To let illusions walk ahead of truth is madness. But to let illusion sink behind the truth and let the truth stand forth as what it is, is merely sanity. (W-155.1,2)

As you can see, there is a great deal more to these two paragraphs, and to the overall lesson, than the simple phrase "the world is an illusion" would suggest on its own. First, both paragraphs, and the lesson as a whole, are speaking of being present in the midst our physical reality in a way that is not illusory, even as those around us may yet perceive in an illusory way. The underlined sections in the quoted passages convey this idea. They speak of reality being "even here" and describe a "way of living in the world that is not here..."

Let's shift to the relevant statement from ACOL: *Or can you not see that the created form was made in God's own image, as was all creation. You are God's image given form, as is all creation.* (C:30.13) It is important to note that ACOL doesn't suggest that the world as we have perceived it to be in the past is in fact an accurate likeness to God, for we have distorted the image with our misperceptions.

Consider this passage: *Each day is your creation held together by the thought system that gave it birth. To observe this is to see its reality. To see this reality is to see the image of God you have created in God's likeness. This image is based on your memory of the truth of God's creation and your desire to create like your Father. It is the best, in your forgetfulness, that you could do; but still it tells you much.* (C:8.24) The passage here suggests that physical reality as we know it is but a facsimile of God's creation. This passage comes relatively early in ACOL, when the core ideas from ACIM are being offered through the language of the heart. In this passage Jesus is speaking about the world as the separated mind has conceived of it. Later in ACOL we come to understand the world we experience is the product of our ideas, beliefs and perceptions—an idea consistent with the teachings of ACIM. As our ideas and beliefs change, so will the world of our experience be transformed, and the New created.

The difficulty here is in desiring to understand the experience of a physical world as being either one thing or the other—as being purely false, and a denial of God's creation, or as being the essence of God's creation and the image of God Himself. Neither is entirely correct, because physical reality is neutral. ACOL says that form in service to illusion reveals and becomes illusion, while form in service to truth reveals and becomes truth.

9. ACIM is clear about everything temporal being illusory. In what sense could I ever be brought to understand that form is divine?

MICHAEL:

First, I think it is important to note that while form itself is described as neutral in ACIM, thoughts and beliefs are not. In ACIM, we are allowed no neutral thoughts, beliefs or perceptions. ACOL agrees: *Nothing is what it is, but only what it is to you.* (ACOL C:3.7) Form itself, being neutral, is thus a blank canvas.

In ACOL, form is described as a representation. What it represents is up to us. Being inherently neutral, form may become a representation of the truth, or it may become a representation of the false. ACOL goes further to suggest that, *A representation of the truth not only reveals the truth, but becomes the truth. A representation of what is not the truth reveals only illusion and becomes illusion.* (ACOL T3:1.4, emphasis added)

A second important point is that ACOL speaks about the One Body of Christ, which is all of form as an undivided whole, the nature of which is *endless.* This is a distinct shift from speaking of individual bodies with which we once mistakenly identified, and which come and go in time, to speaking of the One Whole Body of creation. When viewed this way, it is possible to understand form as both neutral and eternal, and to see that in misperceiving individual forms as being specific and separate beings, we have projected our illusory choice for separation onto form.

Individual bodies come and go, but form itself does not. Form, in wholeness, remains. Our mistake has been to identify with the particular in a way that divides us from one another—to assert that I am this and not that, to assert that I am this body and my fate is tied to it. What is the content of a bird, but Christ? What is the content of a tree, but Christ? And what is the content of the human being, but Christ?

In our separateness we have made form into the evidence of our illusory beliefs. We have made form itself, which is neutral, into a representation of illusion, and all aspects of the world as we understand it—all the rules that seem to bind us, and limit us, and lead to our suffering—are the product of what we have projected onto form itself. But this need not be.

The truth is we don't know what form will be like when our minds are healed, and joined as One, and Jesus asserts some beautiful notions of what a world founded in the extension of truth could be. This topic is difficult to explain fully in a short answer like this, but I would like to emphasize two ideas: first, as we heal, our experience of form may become very different than what it was in the past; and second, ACOL does *not* assert that there is salvation to be found in body identification. It is our minds that are healed, not our bodies. Both ACIM and ACOL are very clear on this point.

Finally I would invite you to consider the following quotations from ACIM, which I feel are aligned with what I have attempted to describe here.

No form endures. It is the thought behind the form of things that lives unchangeable. (ACIM W-187.4)

All thinking produces form at some level. (ACIM T-2.VI.9:14)

The function of thought comes from God and is in God. As part of His Thought, you cannot think apart from Him. (ACIM T-5.V.6:15-16)

10. But I have been told that according to ACIM, the world itself is illusory. Have I misunderstood ACIM? Is ACOL saying something different?

MICHAEL:

As noted in the previous two questions, there is very definitely a condition of perception in which it is accurate to say the world is an illusion. There is also a condition of perception in which the world is not illusory, because it reveals the truth, and in doing so, *becomes* the truth.

To say this simply, the world that we make through the split mind mode of perception is one that literally withers on the vine, while the world that is created through the full and unimpeded extension of the One Mind, of God's Love, and of our own Heart quite literally imbues the neutrality of form with new Life. The passage below from ACOL describes this beautifully.

In order for your body to live, this one Energy had to enter your form and exist where you think you are. This is the Energy of Love, the Energy of Creation, the Source that is known as God. Since you are clearly alive, this Energy exists within you as it exists in all else that lives. It is one Energy endlessly able to materialize in an inexhaustible variety of forms. But form does not contain It and is not required for Its existence or expression. How could form contain God? How could form contain the Energy of Creation?

Your form does not contain your heart, or the energy of creation, or God. Your form is but an extension of this energy, a representation of it. You might think of this as a small spark of the energy that has created a living universe existing within you and uniting you to all that has been created. You are the substance of the universe. The same energy exists in the stars of the heavens and the waters of the ocean that exists in you. This energy is the form and content of the embrace. It is within you and It surrounds and It encompasses you. It is you and all who exist with you. It is the body of Christ. It is like unto what the water of the ocean is to the living matter that exists within it. The living matter that exists within the ocean has no need to search for God. It lives in God. So do you. (ACOL T4:5.4,5)

ACIM suggests that the loveless world seen through the ego's eyes is illusory. ACOL says a world created through the extension of God's Love is real. Both ideas are correct, and it has been our inability to comprehend this beautiful paradox that has prevented us from fully embracing the possibility of Love's fulfillment.

11. ACIM says that the body is an illusion, a miscreation based in fear. ACOL says that the choice to experience a body is simply a choice, a choice that is "consistent with the laws of love." Why this shift?

MICHAEL:

It is important in exploring questions with far-reaching implications such as this that the starting point be as accurate and faithful to the two texts as possible. A search of ACIM, for instance, would not return any quotations in which ACIM says explicitly that the body is in and of itself an illusion or a miscreation. What is clear is that we have tried to make bodies into something they are not through what ACIM describes as *body-identification.*

When we view a specific physical body as the entirety of who we are, then we have clearly misperceived, and the result is illusory. But the body itself is described in ACIM as neutral: *...the body is merely neutral,* (T-20.VII.4:4) and *Time is as neutral as the body is...* (T-26. VIII.3:7)

ACIM also says, *The body is merely part of your experience in the physical world,* (T-2.IV.3:8), *[T]he body is a learning device for the mind,* (T-2.IV.3:1) and *Any thought system that confuses God and the body must be insane.* (T-4.V.3:1) These passages echo the fundamental claim of ACIM regarding the body, which is that it is neutral, as well as a learning device. ACIM also says, *The body is beautiful or ugly, peaceful or savage, helpful or harmful, according to the use to which it is put.* (T-8.VII.4:3)

Passages from ACIM that are very close to the meaning contained in the question—that the body is itself illusory and a miscreation—include these: *God did not make the body, because it is destructible, and therefore not of the Kingdom,* (T-6.V.A.2:1) and *The body is an isolated speck of darkness; a hidden secret room, a tiny spot of senseless mystery, a meaningless enclosure carefully protected, yet hiding nothing.* (T-20.VI.5:2)

A central challenge in reading both Courses is that we are not separate from God, and yet at times Jesus must address the actions and choices that we make from the misperception of separation. This can lead to paradoxes. For instance, if God did not make the body, and we are not truly separate from God, then who or what made them? It is important to consider that a great deal of ACIM is written to minds that have *identified* with the body, and by doing so have made it into a hiding place, *seemingly* separate from God. The mind that has chosen separation thinks the body is all that is real, and because the body becomes such a mind's chosen symbol of its independence from God, it becomes an *isolated speck of darkness.* Such a mind cannot witness the Truth because its forgery would be revealed, so the body with which it had identified becomes a container of nothing at all.

The body performs beautifully its function of enabling a mind that has chosen separation to experience what this means, and to learn from it, and the reason the choice to enter human form is consistent with the laws of Love is because Love knows there is really nothing to fear. Freedom is an integral element of God's kingdom, and to intervene when a simple mistake has been made—such as identifying with the body instead of our eternal home in God's Love—would be to signal that the mistake has genuine consequences. Love allows freedom, but also offers in response the perfect conditions for learning what our choices have meant, that we might make our way home.

Once the mind is freed of body identification new choices and ways of being in relationship to the physical are possible, and these also are simply a choice—but they would no longer be choices made in separation, and the effects of these new choices would be wholly different than the effects of our past choice to try to be separate from God, with our bodies as our own personal kingdoms.

ACOL is not trying to suggest that a physical experience, when conducted in unity and relationship with God, is any better or worse than a mode of being in which we are in formless union with God. But the choice to have a physical experience *with* the knowing of our perfect union with God would transform our experience of this world, and alleviate our suffering. Such a choice would be divine, and powerful, and it would be made as One with our Creator.

12. ACIM says that truth cannot be brought to illusion; rather, illusion must be brought to truth for correction. ACOL's concept of an "elevated Self of form" seems like an attempt to bring truth to illusion. Can you explain?

MICHAEL:

ACIM says this about bringing truth to illusion: *Think you that you can bring truth to fantasy, and learn what truth means from the perspective of illusions? Truth has no meaning in illusion. The frame of reference for its meaning must be itself. When you try to bring truth to illusions, you are trying to make illusions real, and keep them by justifying your belief in them. But to give illusions to truth is to enable truth to teach that the illusions are unreal, and thus enable you to escape from them. Reserve not one idea aside from truth, or you establish orders of reality that must imprison you. There is no order in reality, because everything there is true.* (T-17.I.5:1-7)

First, it is clear to me from this passage that truth cannot be understood from the perspective of illusion. The frame of reference for illusion is completely opposite that of truth. The former begins with body identification and the experience of our seeming separation. The latter is predicated upon genuine knowledge of our Self, and the profound experience of unity with one another and with God. The very words we use can seem to mean different things, depending on the vantage from which we view them.

When we bring truth to illusion, the result is distortion. It may be helpful to consider some examples. We are all chosen by God and have a function to fulfill in the Atonement, as we were all created by God and are extensions of His power and glory. But this does not make us "special" regarding one another. It does not make any of us "anointed" by God to fulfill some secret mission that—just between you and me— God needed "me" to do because I'm just a little bit superior to most everyone else. This is a distortion, and one example of attempting to bring truth to illusion. We each have a function, but it does not make any of us more or less than anyone else.

Another example, which is almost completely opposite in form, is to suggest the physical world is meaningless altogether. The thought goes like this: "Since all the bodies we see are transient, they must not be real, and so it must be the case that we live in a meaningless world." The distortion here is to equate the *content* of reality with the form *first*; and only then, after this distortion has occurred, to say nothing we experience in this world could be meaningful. Meaning is not found in bodies, but nor do bodies preclude us from extending and sharing the light of God within us, from each to each. The distortion that results from bringing truth to illusion in this case is the mindset that the lives we are living today do not matter. This distortion suggests there is no purpose in our relationships to one another, and the result can be a distancing of ourselves from one another, or in the worst case, a depression or complete withdrawal from life itself.

This extreme example comes from attempting to interpret the distinction between truth and falsehood through the lens of illusion. The ego's version of reality does not admit of the possibility that the Kingdom of God *is us*, or that we are truly One in the shared identity of Christ, or that spirit is perfectly whole, eternal and timeless. The attempt to understand the truth Jesus is offering us about our true identity, when examined from the framework of illusion, can produce this type of distortion. Everything "here" (on Earth) is false. Everything "there" (in Heaven) is true. But we are told in ACIM that heaven is not a place, and that ultimately heaven and earth will not exist as separated states, so something is amiss with this type of thinking.

The reason I do not think the "elevated Self of form" is an attempt to bring truth to illusion, is that what is false is the notion of separation, and everything that we made within that framework. What is true is our unity with God, one another, and all Creation.

The body is described as neutral in both ACIM and ACOL, but this neutrality is simply the starting point. In ACOL there is a passage in Chapter 15 of the Dialogues entitled "Becoming and the Principles of Creation" in which Jesus uses the Biblical story of Creation to describe this. He notes that the first step in the Creation story was a mighty wind blowing over the waters and the wasteland. What were these waters? he asks. What was this land?

Jesus answers his own question as follows. *They were barren form. Form unable to create or bear fruit. Form was simply barren form before movement swept across it and animated it with the attention and awareness of spirit—with sound, light, and expression. Could these barren forms not be compared to the forms of the not yet elevated? What if the existence of form was seen to predate the animation of that form with life and spirit? Would this not be consistent with what we attempt to do here? With our continuing work of creation? Would this not even be consistent with spirit existing in every living form from the beginning of time until the end of time?* (D:15.10)

In the paragraph that follows the one quoted above, Jesus says, *Time is what begins and ends. Time is what began when life took on existence in form and space. It is temporal rather than eternal. Alongside it, in the state of unity, rests all that is eternal, all that is real. What is real is but another way of saying what is true. What is true is eternal life, not temporal life. There are no degrees of life. One form is not more alive than another. All that lives contains the breath or wind of spirit, which is eternal and complete.* (D:15.11)

The elevated Self of form is not an attempt to preserve our little, egoic lives that are tied to the body alone, but the elevation of neutral form through the expression of eternal life and the power of Creation. It is not one form that we are interested in, but all of Life itself—as we are One Body in Christ. Our fundamental identification is with eternal reality, not a self that begins and ends with the limitations of our body. This is very different from attempting to bring truth to illusion.

The Role of Mind, Heart, Feeling, and Relationship

13. ACOL puts a huge emphasis on "wholeheartedness." What is meant by that?

MICHAEL:

Wholeheartedness is the unity of heart and mind. ACOL says: *The first move toward wholeness is but to understand this: heart and mind are not separate. A united mind and heart is a whole heart, or wholeheartedness. You may ask then why this Course has treated them as separate parts of you. This is simply because this is the way you see them, and because it has allowed me to address the different functions you have given them.* (C:17.17)

But what then is wholeheartedness? It is one of those words that Jesus suggests in ACOL describes a reality that cannot be taught, like Love itself.

I liken the condition of *not* being wholehearted, as being one in which the knowing of our hearts and the beliefs of our mind are in conflict. Like the moment when a child attends the theater for the first time, and intuitively says, "I am going to be an actor!" and the parent says, protectively, knowing the harsh realities of this world, "This is foolishness! Such a road will lead only to suffering. Something more practical is required." This type of conflict occurs within each of us, all the time, whenever we occupy what ACIM describes as the split mind condition.

To *not* be wholehearted is to be powerless. In wholeheartedness, we are whole, unified, eternal, powerful, and creative.

SUSAN:

While both ACIM and ACOL are meant to eradicate the ego and return us to Christ-consciousness, Jesus says that ACIM only threatened the ego enough to loosen its hold, but not eradicate it altogether. Our world today is evidence. There is hope! Jesus reminds us of our power, and the miracle that can transform our world.

You do not realize what a wholehearted choice in regards to experiencing separation did. Wholeheartedness is but a full expression of your power. A full expression of your power is creation. What has been created cannot be uncreated. What has been created can, however, be transformed. Transformation occurs in time. Thus transformation and miracles need to work hand-in-hand. (C:18.18)

ACOL leads us to the ego's demise, and the end of separation. Jesus appeals to our hearts and through them we, and thus the world, become transformed. The Prelude concludes with: *This time we take a direct approach, an approach that seems at first to leave behind abstract learning and the complex mechanisms of the mind that so betray you. We take a step away from the intellect, the pride of the ego, and approach this final learning through the realm of the heart.* (P.44)

Though we turn our minds toward our hearts we can't avoid the mind altogether, but we turn away from pure intellect, and join heart and mind in what Jesus calls "wholeheartedness."

Love appeals to you through the heart. God appeals to you through your heart. Your heart has not been open to the appeals of love partially because of your use of concepts. Concepts have been used to order your world and to assist your mind in keeping track of all that is in it. Your mind does not need this assistance. To begin to conceptualize in ways that touch your heart will free your mind of its reliance on thought concepts, thus allowing your heart and mind <u>to speak the same language or to be communicated with in the same way.</u> (C:21.4 emphasis in original)

It can come as no surprise to you that your mind has ruled your heart. What this Course has thus far attempted to do is to briefly change your orientation from mind to heart. This is the first step in what will seem now like an attempt to balance two separate things, but is really an attempt to unite what you have only perceived as separate. If the heart is the center of your Self, where then is the mind? The center is but the Source in which all exist as one mind. To say this to you before we loosened some of your perceptions about the supremacy of the mind, however, would have been folly. The one mind is not as you have perceived <u>your</u> mind. The one mind is but a mind in which love rules, *and mind and heart are one. We will proceed by calling this whole-heartedness rather than mind or heart.* (C:18.16 emphasis in original)

To some extent we identify with our thoughts. While ACIM separated us from our thoughts and the meaning we attached to them, ACOL takes us beyond mind to a new kind of "thought." It is a way of thought in which mind and heart work together in a united function.

A recurring theme in ACOL is joining. The introduction of fear into the mind of God's son created all problems. To heal what seems many problems there is one solution: forgiveness, which rests on joining in wholeness, or Oneness. In ACIM the end of separation was called Atonement. Atonement is achieved through forgiveness. Similarly, in ACOL Jesus introduces forgiveness and joining, stating that, *Joining rests on forgiveness.* (C:6)

This first joining in unity, the joining of heart and mind, joins the physical and spiritual world in a relationship of which you can be more and more steadily aware. It is a new relationship. Unity always existed. Oneness always existed. God always existed. But you separated yourself from direct awareness of your <u>relationship</u> with unity, with oneness, with God, just as you separated yourself from relationship with the wholeness of the pattern of creation. You have believed in God and perhaps some concept of unity or oneness, but you have also denied even the possibility of experiencing your own direct relationship with God, or the possibility that your life is a direct experience of the pattern of unity or oneness that is creation. (T4:2.22 emphasis in original)

Thus the integration of mind and heart must be our goal in order for you to create the state in which unity can be experienced. (C:18.15)

Learning from unity requires an integrated mind and heart, or wholeheartedness. (C:18.9)

We perceived the mind and heart as separate and considered the mind superior to heart. A wholeheart, or mind and heart joined, is the one mind we share with all.

The separated self cannot relearn unity except through union. (C:19.10, 12)

Do not forget what union is. Union is the mind and heart being joined in wholeheartedness. (T1:6.4)

It is only in combining mind and heart with a focus on letting the heart lead that love can be combined with thought in such a way as to actually transcend thought as you know it. This transcendence is a function of wholeheartedness. (C:19.13)

We cannot know God, the truth, peace, or our Selves through learning in separation. We need to learn anew the meaning of what it means to be a Child of God. We can't learn through the experience of others, even Jesus himself. The only way to learn as the Christ and to create a new world, is through unity which arises from wholeheartedness. *What happens when this oneness is accomplished is that divine memories arise to replace perception. This is miracle-mindedness. The accomplishment of this state of being is the reason for which you are here. It is your return to your Self. It heralds the return of heaven through the second coming of Christ, the energy that will bridge the two worlds.* (T1:6.9)

Make a new choice! The choice that your heart yearns to make for you and that your mind is finding increasingly difficult to deny. When you choose unity over separation, you choose reality over illusion. (C:6.5)

This choice begins with joining mind and heart in wholeheartedness. It is only a beginning. Wholeheartedness requires Jesus' guidance to recognize this state, and to identify wholehearted responses. We fell into forgetfulness and lost our way by trying to understand of our circumstances with a split mind. We must now remember the truth about who we are. With Jesus' help, and a mind and heart joined, we can create a new world. The following passages give us a glimpse into the profound change that comes from wholeheartedness. *The heart and mind joined in union accomplished the reunion of the separated self with God. The resurrection was evidence of this accomplishment. It laid aside death's claim and with it the claim of all that is temporary.* (T1:8.8) And: *Illusion is the death you need arise from. Arise and awaken to your resurrected self! There is no longer a* <u>god-head</u> *to follow into paradise. Take not the example of any of these and know instead the example of woman, of Mary, Mother of God.* (T1:8.9, orig. emphasis)

Mary becomes the example life to follow in the creation of the new world. Like Mary, we are called to return to our virgin state where the new pattern of life is the ability to resurrect in form, in life, now. *Thus is the glory that is yours returned to you in_life rather than in_death.* (T1:8.15, emphasis in original) All this comes, and begins, when we join heart and mind in wholeheartedness.

14. Does ACOL denigrate the mind?

GLENN:

No, it gives the mind a different purpose. ACIM is a course in mind training. *It would be very intelligent of you to set yourself the goal of really studying for this course.* (COA ed., T-4.VII.10)

ACOL asks for every bit as much diligence, but uses a dramatically different approach. The very first words of the Introduction say: *This course was written for the mind—but only to move the mind to appeal to the heart. To move it to listen. To move it to accept confusion. To move it to cease its resistance to mystery, its quest for answers, and to shift its focus to the truth and away from what can be learned only by the mind.* (C:I.1)

The problem with the human mind, ACOL says, is that it creates mental constructs which then tell you how to feel according to its rules. *The mind so hates to be confused, to be open, to remain open, and to not know. . . The mind cannot hold open the doors of the heart and yet we turn within, turn to the mind, and show it where its openness lies, where sweetness abides, where love's knowing is found. . . The heart is needed to guide the mind in a way that it does not desire to be guided, a way that is one of joining, a way that does not allow the mind's separate stance, its rules, or its right answers.* (C:I.4-6)

ACOL says it seeks to "bypass" the mind—a word it uses no less than four times, such as here: *Despite whatever method you feel you used to learn what you have learned, what this Course did was bypass the way of learning of the ego and call upon the Christ in you to learn anew.* (T3:15.13)

15. ACIM says that pain is the result of guilt, whereas ACOL says that pain is the result of feelings of lack of love. Why the difference?

MICHAEL:

For me there is no real difference between the idea of guilt, as presented in ACIM, and the idea of lack of love. Guilt in ACIM is the feeling of the ego, born of the choice for separation, and the dim recognition that this choice of ours is the cause of our suffering. Guilt is simply what belief in an ego feels like. But what are the consequences of the choice for separation but the seeming lack of love? This is why, for me, the two are synonymous.

16. I have the impression that ACOL deals a lot with feelings and emotions. Is this true?

GLENN:

Both ACIM and ACOL speak of feelings. Please see Michael's discussion below. I address only ACOL's contribution to this important topic. One might say that feelings are every bit as significant as thought, and more difficult to address. It might be helpful to break this topic into three sections.

✠ **Let's start with negative feelings.**

Actually, let's start with something distinctive to ACOL: **bitter** feelings. ACOL makes a stunning statement: *Bitterness is to your heart what the ego has been to your mind. . . [I]t has become, like the ego, so much a part of your reality that it must, like the ego, be consciously left behind.* (T3:6.5) Thus bitter feelings, ACOL says, are a kind of emotional equivalent of the ego, *a source of resistance as strong as that of the ego and more deeply felt,* (T3:8.3,4) and rivals only the ego itself in destructiveness.

Bitterness arises from the belief that one's virtues have gone unrecognized, or from feeling passed over for reward, or for thinking that one has not received one's due credit or honor. It's built upon the perception that something has gone "wrong" in the universe, that we have unjustly been made to suffer. It arises among religious people who *believe in a savior who could have, but did not, keep you from this suffering.* (T3:8.5) Bitterness also arises from the helpless feeling arising when we want to, but do not feel able, to relieve the suffering of others. Bitterness and blame, in turn, are associated with the desire for revenge.

ACOL cultivates its opposite, the condition of tenderness, from which the choice to leave bitterness behind can be made. ACOL says that it must *be consciously left behind.* (T3:6.5) One recognizes one's own bitterness and makes a different choice.

✠ **And yet, ACOL says there are no "bad" feelings. What are we to do with our feelings?**

We might assume that negative feelings arise from the ego, yet ACOL says that <u>all</u> feeling comes from love.

Your feelings in truth come from love, your response to them is what is guided by fear. Even feelings of destruction and violence come from love. You are not bad, and you have no feelings that can be labeled so. Yet you are misguided concerning what your feelings mean and how they would bring love to you and you to love. (C:5.11) It is the separated self that labels right or wrong, good or bad. Nevertheless, we all have feelings that are uncomfortable and seem unloving. What is to be done with them?

First of all, it's critical to understand what is not being asked: *This is not about acceptance of what you do not like. Do you really think you are being called to accept "normal life?" ... [Y]ou are not called to accept what you do not like, but to accept that you don't like whatever it is you don't like. Then, and only then—when you have accepted how you feel—can you respond truly.* (D:Day8.3,4)

In addition, ACOL does <u>not</u> say that we need to express outwardly all our feelings, which may not necessarily be helpful or healing.

So what is to be done with feelings? ACOL says, *[B]ring the thoughts and feelings that arise to the place within your heart that has been prepared for them. You do not deny them. You bring them first to your Self, to the Self joined in unity at the place of your heart. From this place you learn to discriminate, to separate the false from the true, for your ego thoughts cannot long abide in the holy place of your heart. Then, with truth and illusion separated, you develop the discipline to express your true Self, as you are now.* (T2:7.19) Thus it is within the spaciousness of the heart that our feelings can be alchemized and transformed, and clarity can be known.

ACOL repeatedly emphasizes that feelings are not to be denied or repressed because there is "no escape" from feelings, even long-buried ancient feelings. They are merely buried. They still exist and must be re-integrated into the One Self. The re-integration process, ACOL promises, will be *proof of the benevolence of your feelings and of the benevolence of the universe itself.* (D:Day16.7)

Jesus acknowledges that this process may be difficult, but becomes easier with practice. It is a prerequisite for the condition of unity.

✠ Feelings are a doorway to God.

Although feelings are often problematic, ACOL urges the reader not to fear feelings but to accept them as a "helpmate" coming from the body when the body has been given a new purpose. But the key is acceptance, not rejection, of feelings. Non-acceptance but continues the separation. Acceptance requires one to be fully "in the present" with whatever feelings arise. These feelings need to be allowed to arise in one's awareness and be held in the heart like a beloved, upset child.

[Y]our feelings are not misleading you but supporting you! That they are but calling you to expression of your true Self! (D:Day8.28) A true response holds all feelings, even feelings such as anger, in acceptance and an embrace of love.

Feelings, like thoughts, are creative. They have power beyond our imaginings. *When feelings are shown, or made visible, the new is created. . . Each blade of grass, each flower, each stone, is a creation of feelings. All you need do is look about you to know that feelings of love still abound. Beauty still reigns.* (D:Day18.11)

Michael:

Both ACIM and ACOL work with feelings. In ACIM, feelings are often used as a guidepost for what we have chosen to value. Our feelings tell us how we perceive ourselves, and how we interpret the present moment. ACIM says, *It is obvious that any situation that causes you concern is associated with feelings of inadequacy, for otherwise you would believe that you could deal with the situation successfully.* (W-47.5:2) Also, *The continuing decision to remain separated is the only possible reason for continuing guilt feelings.* (T-5.V.8:1) And, *Yet we have learned that the idea of death takes many forms. It is the one idea which underlies all feelings that are not supremely happy.* (W-167.2:3) In truth our feelings have always been our guide, for peace is not something that we can process logically.

As with many aspects of ACIM's emphasis on teaching through contrast, I think that we sometimes have taken ideas too far. If our feelings reveal to us how we have chosen to perceive ourselves and one another, and we discover that we have feelings of guilt, anxiety, or depression, then we can know from the teachings of ACIM that we have misperceived. It would be appropriate, I think, for us to explore our beliefs and thought processes in order to find where we have accepted as true, ideas that are not true. Without the mind training provided in ACIM, and the help of the Holy Spirit to assist us in denying the veracity of what these feelings *appear* to tell us, we would be lost to our own feelings. For when we are feeling depressed, or guilty, or inadequate, the feeling seems to be telling us that this is so. But these feeling are not actually telling us what is so—they are telling us what we have chosen! In this sense, they are a perfect learning device.

We overlearn when we question our feelings and move into an intellectual mode of perceiving. We then discount the wisdom of our feelings and remove ourselves from the full range of intelligence they offer. We observe this occurring when the mind "tells us" how to feel. This involves a subtle form of judgment, in which the mind imposes a particular interpretation onto the experience of the present and then tries to assert what we "ought" to be feeling.

A primary objective of ACOL is to assist us in unifying the heart and mind, so that we can give a wholehearted response to what is. A wholehearted response is spontaneous and loving—unique to each encounter and situation—and this simply cannot occur while we are engaged in the practice of "trying" to feel a particular way, or "deciding" how we should be feeling.

An important realization for me was that once we have accepted who we truly are, then our feelings cannot mislead us. If we find ourselves feeling grief or sorrow at the sight of a starving child, it doesn't mean that we have sided with the ego, it simply offers us an opportunity to respond. And in wholeheartedness we not only *know* that we are capable of giving a response, we know that our feelings have called us to respond, and we know that our response comes from Love.

The response of wholeheartedness is never based on the ego's thought system of body identification, but on the pure, free knowing of what we would offer from the infinite well of our One Heart. Our response, in wholeheartedness, is the movement of God through us, as us. I think, at times, the teachings of ACIM, when taken too far, have resulted in some of us withholding the power of our own response through the judgment of the very feelings that call upon the offering of Love that only we can give.

17. When reading ACOL, there is such an emphasis on "relationship" – not only to other people but to everything. Why is relationship such a big deal?

MICHAEL:

To answer this question, it is necessary to entertain a paradox. We know from ACIM that the Sonship was created by the Father as an extension of Himself. The paradox is this: the Sonship neither exists separately from the Father, nor is the Sonship perfectly identical with the Father. A distinction exists without separation, which is Creation.

Relationship is, in essence, the glue that allows for distinction without separation. I like to think of relationship as that which is identical to all that exists—that holy, nameless presence of God that exists within each of us and every element of Creation. That presence is the heart of everything. Its presence in each of us and all that exists is what "relates" us to one another in a profound, eternal, and unbreakable way. It is this relatedness that links us each to each, indelibly. Without this fundamental identity with one another, we would be truly separate, and this, we know, cannot be so.

In ACIM this idea is presaged with the notion of communication. Consider this passage: *Existence as well as being rest on communication. Existence, however, is specific in how, what and with whom communication is judged to be worth undertaking. Being is completely without these distinctions. It is a state in which the mind is in communication with everything that is real. To whatever extent you permit this state to be curtailed you are limiting your sense of your own reality, which becomes total only by recognizing all reality in the glorious context of its real relationship to you. This is your reality. Do not desecrate it or recoil from it. It is your real home, your real temple and your real Self.* (T-4.VII.4:1-8) I would recommend reading the preceding paragraph in ACIM as well, to see the way in which ACIM describes creation and communication as synonymous.

But also, Creation involves distinction. I live in Maine, and you live in Utah. This does not mean we are separate. But it does mean we are distinct from one another in this way. In ACOL such distinctions are described as attributes, as noted previously. It is precisely because of our fundamental relatedness that we are each able to take on differing attributes without becoming separate. We remain One Mind, One Body, and One Heart, even as we differentiate through the divine process of Creation in order to express who we are to one another, and to perpetually deepen and extend the varieties and forms of expression. Creation is a celebration of who we are, and always will be.

Relationship not only binds us all together as One, it allows us to differentiate. Differentiation has no meaning without relatedness. If you had a Universe all to yourself that was blue, and I had a Universe all to myself that was red, and we were truly separate, then red and blue would be meaningless. They would be the everything and nothing of our separate little kingdoms. It is only because God maintains the fundamental unity, or Oneness, of all that exists, that red and blue are enabled to exist in relationship to one another. It is the relatedness of all to all that enables the divine process of Creation to exist at all.

18. Does ACOL treat gender issues differently from ACIM?

GLENN:

Although ACOL generally uses the masculine pronoun, its terminology is inclusive of the feminine—it speaks of sons and daughters, she's and he's. It is welcoming of any sexual orientation: *[T]his call to return to your Self is being sounded far and wide and . . . goes out to humble and ordinary people like yourself. There is no exclusivity to this call. It excludes no race nor religion nor ones of either sex or sexual preference. It but calls all to love and to live in the abundance of the truth.* (T3:21.21)

ACOL also speaks of Mary, the mother of Jesus, and a feminine "Way of Mary" that exists in symbiotic relationship to the "Way of Jesus" now ending: *Christ-consciousness was represented not only by Jesus, but by his mother, Mary. Mary, like Jesus, realized full Christ-consciousness and full expression of Christ-consciousness in form. Each did so in individual ways, ways that revealed the choices available to those who would follow after them.* (D:Day17.9)

Learning vs. Knowing, and the End of Learning

Note: The ACOL theme of "the end of learning" progresses from a time when the ego's thought system is weakened yet learning is still needed, to new ways of learning, to moving beyond learning by accepting the truth of who we are.

19. ACOL tells us that "the time of learning" is over. What does this mean?

LAUREL:

Learning is a mind activity that has helped you skillfully navigate your human experience through adding information and memories to your knowledge base. Learning was very important to your human experience and even to your spiritual journey. You learned about religions, spiritual practices, and spiritual teachings. You even learned that no amount of learning brought you lasting happiness. In bringing you here, to the point of discovery, learning has accomplished its goal and can be set aside. When ACOL declares that the time of learning is finished, it invites you to replace the activity of learning with the activity of discovery.

In discovery, the heart's recognition is prioritized over the mind's accumulation and regurgitation of past knowledge. Learning expanded and strengthened the separated mind. Discovery expands the heart. Accumulated knowledge is not useful to present moment discovery because it is founded on the past. It is set aside as you come into the present moment to discover what is true. Like a child setting off on an adventure into the forest, you don't know what you'll find because you haven't discovered it yet. If you insist on relying on the past, your exploration will just be a reiteration of past conclusions, and nothing real will be seen.

In separation, the mind is in control. Occasional input from the heart is allowed, but is often overridden by logic and analysis. In discovery, these positions are reversed. The heart is in the driver's seat, with the mind in its natural position as a reference tool for practical matters. Discovery insists on a fresh, open mind without preconceived ideas. Living from discovery is life on the edge of your seat, free from the past with open inclusion of whatever is true right now. Discovery is entering into relationship with the vibrancy of this moment and this experience.

ACOL teaches that we've exhausted the usefulness of accumulating more information. We turn toward our whole experience, joining a moment that is fluid and unprecedented. Discovery moves beyond identification as a small, separated human being to embrace our whole Being while enjoying a unique and personal differentiated experience. This is the reason for differentiation and is available to you now through discovery.

MICHAEL:

One of the conditions of learning is an incomplete knowledge, or acceptance, of our true nature. Learning is an aid to facilitating our remembrance of who we truly are. Once this is accomplished, learning is complete. There is no more knowledge to be gained.

But Creation is not over, for Creation was never about learning per se. It was about creating—sharing and revealing the content of who we truly are, and who God is. The creative experiences we have when learning is complete are no longer intended to assist us in remembering what we had forgotten about ourselves, but in sharing in ever new and ever-expanding ways the truth of who we are. Nothing we experience once learning is complete will ever change our knowledge of who we are, but it deepens our awareness and joy of who we are. This is discovery. We will never again be mistaken about ourselves or one another, but we may be joyously and profoundly surprised by the endless depth of the beauty and grace that lives in us.

20. ACIM speaks of how entrenched the ego is. ACOL tells the reader that "the ego-self is gone." Why this big shift?

SUSAN:

The goal of ACIM has always been the eradication of our belief in the "ego-self," or the personal self. The ego believes that it is alone; separate from others, from God, and from everything else in the world. In ACIM Jesus says of the ego:

What is the ego? Nothingness, but in a form that seems like something. In a world of form the ego cannot be denied for it alone seems real. Yet could God's Son as He created him abide in form or in a world of form? Who asks you to define the ego and explain how it arose can be but he who thinks it real.... (C-2.2)

The coursework of ACOL furthers the aim of ACIM. In the Prelude to ACOL Jesus states:

The world as a state of being, as a whole, has entered a time, brought on largely by A Course in Miracles, in which readiness for miracle-mindedness was upon it. A Course in Miracles opened a door by threatening the ego. All those who, with egos weakened, walked this world with the hope of leaving ego behind, with miracle-minded intent, have awakened human beings to a new identity. (C:P.5)

ACIM introduced us to the ability of the light of truth to dispel darkness, and revealed the ego as nothingness:

Where there was darkness now we see the light. What is the ego? What the darkness was. Where is the ego? Where the darkness was. What is it now and where can it be found? Nothing and nowhere. Now the light has come: its opposite has gone without a trace. (C-2.6)

Jesus intended us to overcome the ego through ACIM. Recognizing that we did not, he tries again. This time by way of the heart. In this final learning, he appeals to us through the heart, and we discover who we are in truth. The journey through ACOL is personal. The abolishment of the ego occurs through a process of learning and unlearning and an individualized transformation that re-establishes true identity. The joining of mind and heart in wholeheartedness returns this to our awareness. Shining the light of the truth on the darkness of the ego dispels it altogether. Take Jesus's hand and again, resign as your own teacher. Take the journey of personal transformation, and you will join others who have entered the time of Christ.

Now that you know who you are in truth, the ego does not remain, with a separate life of its own. No. The ego is gone. Because it was a lie its exposure to the truth dissolved it. (D:5.8)

21: ACOL asks us to "learn in a new way." Is it really new?

LAUREL:

The workbook of ACIM frequently uses guided inquiry to challenge existing beliefs. Example: *I give this chair all the meaning it has for me. I am not angry for the reasons I think.* It also introduces the idea that we are able to choose our responses: *I could choose peace instead of this.*

These inquiries do much to pave the way for the shift offered in ACOL. After ACIM, we can never view the world in the same way again. We recognize its illusory nature, having looked the conditioned ego in the face. ACIM works to un-do our habitual responses and conclusions. It questions the conventional view of reality. It reignites love as the voice of the Holy Spirit. These understandings are huge, and ACOL is not in conflict with any of it.

The "new way" to learn in ACOL moves away from ideas, toward action. This action is most frequently called "joining," but other words for this activity are "love" and "union." Joining is a present moment experience rather than a mental concept or belief. Beyond a theory or intellectual understanding of oneness, this way of learning is always open-ended and undiscovered. It requires present moment willing-ness to explore and engage with whatever is present. Joining is an activity outside of time. It bridges your unique differentiated experi-ence with the one love that supports and creates all. While knowledge can be accumulated, joining is always completely fresh and is beyond the intellect.

Since the voice of the Holy Spirit has now been assimilated and inte-grated, its guidance is a constant partner in navigating the experience at hand. Logic, analysis, and comparison, as key tools of the mind, are no longer dominant. Inner guidance is the navigator. Present moment acceptance is key. Joining what *is* is our new way of dancing with life. This kind of "learning" can't be stored or accumulated, but it is alive and transformative.

MICHAEL:

ACIM describes itself as a course in mind training, as noted previ-ously. For us to recognize the distinction between truth and illusion, it was necessary for us to become aware of the contrast between the two. While our minds remain in conflict due to our belief in separa-tion, this contrast is one of the most essential teaching vehicles of the Holy Spirit. But this emphasis on contrast was described in ACIM as a temporary one.

ACIM says, *You will not remember change and shift in Heaven. You have need of contrast only here. Contrast and differences are neces-sary teaching aids, for by them you learn what to avoid and what to seek. When you have learned this, you will find the answer that makes the need for any differences disappear.* (T-13.XI.6)

Here we see that the idea of contrast is only a temporary aid. Once we discover the Truth, such distinctions dissolve in our recognition of Oneness. Part of the new way of learning in ACOL is through releasing the knowledge that has always been within, in our heart(s). The following paragraphs from ACOL describe this, and they note as well that this learning mode is no longer about contrast.

These words of love do not enter your body through your eyes and take up residence in your brain, there to be distilled into a language that you can understand. As you read, be aware your heart, for this is where this learning enters and will stay. Your heart is now your eyes and ears. Your mind can remain within your concept of the brain, for we bypass it now and send it no information to process, no data for it to compute. The only change in thinking you are asked to make is to realize that you do not need it.

What this will mean to you goes far beyond the learning of this Course. One such concept, given up and not replaced, will free you beyond your deepest imaginings and free your sisters and brothers as well. Once one such concept is felled, others follow quickly. But none is more entrenched than this one, the one we begin today to let fall away.

You who have been unable to separate mind from body, brain from head, and intelligence from knowledge, take heart. We give up trying. We simply learn in a new way and in our learning realize that our light shines from within our heart, our altar to the Lord. Here the Christ in us abides and here we concentrate our energies and our learning, soon to learn that what we would know cannot be computed in the databanks of an over-worked and over-trusted brain, a mind we cannot separate from where we believe it to be. (C:3.14-16)

We see here one of the reasons we have been given ACOL—to provide us with an alternate means of learning that bypasses the thinking mind. When we were entrenched in the ego's thought system, it was necessary for us to learn new concepts. Once adopted, such concepts provide us with a glimpse of the contrast that exists between truth and illusion. The thinking mind was the only place for us to begin, because it was the primary means we used to understand the world.

There is a limit on this mode of learning, however, and that is this: it is all too easy for concepts given to us as leading indicators of the contrast that exists between truth and illusion to be made into a rigid formula by the thinking mind. In short, it is all too easy for the thinking mind to assert its authority, without affording the heart the opening that is required for its return to its rightful place in our being. The thinking mind, separated from the heart, can never be whole, and so long as we identify with the thinking mind alone, a most important part of us remains missing. The heart, after all, is where our treasure lies: *Remember that where your heart is, there is your treasure also.* (T-2.II.1:5)

22. ACOL holds out the possibility of "direct learning." How does this happen?

LAUREL:

Begin by considering the opposite prospect, "indirect learning." By definition, indirect learning must be learning that comes through an outside source. We read about it, hear about it, or are taught about it through someone else. It is not something we have ourselves discovered, but we have received information through a trusted source. That doesn't mean that what we have learned is not meaningful to us. We may value what we have learned, and our understanding may have been richly expanded.

Consider the metaphor of learning about an island we have never before visited. Indirect learning offers knowledge about the island from other reliable sources. We can read about the island in books, look at pictures of the island, attend lectures and see slide shows of others who have been to the island, and watch videos or travel shows about the island. This is indirect learning.

Direct learning happens when we actually go to the island ourselves. We explore the waterfalls and villages firsthand. We feel the spray of the waterfall against our skin. We see the sand on the beach under our own toes and smell the seaweed that has washed ashore. We taste the local food and meet the indigenous people. We know the island in a deeper way because we experience it firsthand through our own senses. Our acquired indirect knowledge may enhance our intellectual understanding of the island and its history, but it only supplements our direct experience.

This firsthand discovery of joining is the new direct learning ACOL offers. ACOL is the guidebook you use to help you explore the island yourself. It can help you choose your experiences and direct you to the places that enrich your understanding. You do the actual experiencing. You do the discovering. You are the one who is changed through what you see.

Direct learning is not only possible, it has the potential to be ongoing. In an interactive and responsive creation, direct engagement with your differentiated experience nurtures a loving and cooperative relationship with all of life and offers continual discovery of life's infinite expressions.

23. ACOL tells us that "the time of the Holy Spirit" is over. Please explain.

LAUREL:

The term "Holy Spirit" is used to describe the intermediary Voice that serves as translator between humans and God. It is the Holy Spirit who reminds us of truth when we are lost in separation. Traditional Christianity identifies three components of God as "Father, Son, and Holy Spirit." When we believe ourselves to be separated beings, the Holy Spirit and the Father are seen as "something other than me." Communication comes from the Father via the Holy Spirit to the Son. The Son does not have direct access. The Holy Spirit is needed as an intermediary. It comes from beyond what I identify as "me."

ACOL invites us to directly experience our unity with all of creation. We discover that we are not separate from Source or from each other. There is One energy, One love, One Being. As oneness is discovered, there is no longer any need to package our connection to Source through a mysterious Holy Spirit outside ourselves. We have continuous, direct access to the One Being because we are it. The beautiful, loving energy of the Holy Spirit isn't gone. Nothing has changed except the boundaries we ourselves have constructed. Without the perception of separation from the Father, we expand our capacity to embrace our direct access to the Source.

This is not an inflated ego, claiming to be God. This is an action; it is joining in place of separating, Oneness in place of other-ness, and stepping into our own two shoes as God/Man, a Christ, One Being in differentiated relationship with its expressions.

MICHAEL:

Part of the need for the Holy Spirit was our entrenchment in the ego's mode of perceiving—the self-fulfilling prophecy of projecting, experiencing, and thus believing ideas about ourselves and our condition that simply were not correct. So deeply have we been ensnared by the ego's mandates, direct contact with reality has simply not been possible. One reason the time of the Holy Spirit is over, as described in ACOL, is that we have substantially been released from the ego's thought system, and direct contact is now possible. We were never intended to exist in the condition of learning forever, and the end of the time of the Holy Spirit coincides with the completion of our healing.

24. Many people have set themselves up as ACIM teachers. ACOL seems almost "beyond teaching." Is this true?

LAUREL:

Jesus' life is the example life, and one of his roles was as a teacher. He offered himself as a public figure so that people could experience firsthand the presence of someone who was awake. He also taught new ideas that changed the world, ideas like love, forgiveness, and a God of compassion.

ACOL teaches that the Way of Jesus is coming to a close. This makes perfect sense because knowledge is of limited use to the spiritual aspirant. What information can be learned indirectly through a teacher that is as powerful as your own direct experience? The days of projecting responsibility for your spiritual fulfillment onto another are finished. There is no need for a guru to transmit information for you because you yourself have direct access.

This doesn't mean that we stop talking to each other, or that inquiry guides can't be helpful. What it does mean is that the only "teachers" that serve you now are those who point you back to yourself. There is no hierarchy between teachers and students. All teach through our example lives, and we all learn through Self-discovery. Those guides or teachers who encourage you to discover your own experience are brothers and sisters who have been guided to share their journeys. They don't want to be separated and set above. Out of love and recognition of your sacredness, they point the way to your own access.

It is the ego that seeks more knowledge, hoping that more knowledge will fix the identity and finally figure out this world. That is a losing game. The ego can never be fixed because it is based on the false idea of separation. No accumulation of knowledge will ever rescue you from a separated world. Only firsthand recognition of your Self can bring you happiness and reveal your true place in creation. Recognition can't be taught by anyone, but it can be experienced by you. Other people may reflect your Self back to you, but they serve only as mirrors and reminders of your own Self. Since there is One Being, all expressions are the beloved, with equal access to the One love that supports and expresses through us all.

MICHAEL:

There are conceptual understandings and core ideas in both Courses that may be taught and learned. The important thing to understand is that intellectual understanding of what may be conceptually understood is *not* the same as release from the dream of separation. In ACOL there is deliberate movement away from the mind-training given in ACIM, and emphasis on *receiving* and *discovering*, rather than learning.

We struggle mightily with such an instruction, for we have been conditioned to think that anything we've ever accomplished or gained has been the product of our own efforts, without which we would have gained nothing. When we experience ourselves as lacking in any way, or as "needing" further development or growth or insight, we thus set about to make an effort at acquiring it. But this effort is ultimately ineffectual, for we do not have the power or authority to give ourselves what we ultimately desire, and God has already given it to us, as us. Further effort only displaces our acceptance of what has already been given, because the very effort is a statement of our lack.

There are concepts we can learn from a study of ACOL, but further conceptual understanding is not the aim of the Course. Jesus says that we might learn conceptually, and realize modest improvements in the condition of our lives, but that this will not bring about the transformation we truly desire in our hearts. It will not bring the Heaven we seek. It is not ACOL that is beyond teaching, it is Love and wholeheartedness that are beyond conceptual understanding.

The teacher-student relationship as historically practiced is one that places an intermediary between the student and God, and what is necessary for our shift out of the time of learning and into the fully-realized truth of who we are is a direct experience of the truth. So long as we continue to place an intermediary, in whatever form, between ourselves and the knowledge of our own hearts, for just as long do we displace the completion of our return to genuine knowledge.

For this reason, the emphasis in ACOL for those who may seek to physically join in groups and share the material with one another is on shared discovery, through dialogue, in which all participants are equal pioneers in the territory of our One Heart. The emphasis in ACOL is not on teaching per se, or debating conceptual understanding, but on sharing experiences, by which we inspire one another to the memory of what is true in all of us.

Significant and Distinctive Terms Used in ACOL

25. ACOL speaks a lot of "the New." What is meant by the New?

GUEST CONTRIBUTOR LYNN KIDD:

What is "New" in ACOL is the wondrous invitation of a "sustained" Christ Consciousness, which conceivably could be one continuous "Holy Instant." In ACIM, we were told that this has never happened. *The world has not yet experienced any comprehensive reawakening or rebirth. Such a rebirth is impossible as long as you continue to project or miscreate. It still remains within you, however, to extend as God extended His Spirit to you.* (T-2.I.3:7-9)

Yet ACOL sounds the call: *What you are called to do is to, through your multitude, sustain Christ-consciousness, and thus create the union of the human and the divine as a new state of being. This union will take you beyond the goal of expressing your Self in form because this goal but reflected the desire for a temporary experience.* (T4:4.18)

Thus the "individuated" Christ nature becomes observable in form as the "elevated Self of form" of which ACOL speaks, and so becomes a spacious, loving, and receptive presence that makes known our shared identity in Christ.

MICHAEL:

The New is a concept introduced in ACOL that is not easily explained outside of the Course itself, but it also has roots in ACIM. We might think of time spent in the dream of separation as nothing at all—a blip in the eternal flow of Creation—and that the New will be all that we create upon our return to knowledge, in union and relationship with God, with all that is, and with one another.

The New is both a return to the beginning—to the moment of our creation by God, to perfect union with God and to the *knowing* of that perfect union—as well as the birth of what has never been, for Creation is not static. It is ever-moving into new forms of expression, even as the Knowledge and Truth at its center are changeless. The New, in other words, is creation.

It is best perhaps, to offer ACOL's vision of the new, in the words of the Course.

Creation of the new has begun. We are an interactive part of this creative act of a loving Creator. Creation is a dialogue. Creation— which is God and us in unity—will respond to our responses. Will respond to what we envision, imagine and desire. Creation of the new could not begin without you. Your willingness for the new, a willingness that included the leaving behind of the old, a willingness that included the leaving behind of fear and judgment and a separate will, was necessary to begin creation of the new. Your former willingness to accept the old but kept creation's power harnessed to the old. Does this not make perfect sense when you realize that creation, like God, is not "other than" who you are? How could creation proceed on to the new without you?

What will the future hold? It is up to us dear brothers and sisters. It is up to us acting as one body, one mind, one heart. It is up to us creating as one body, one mind, one heart. Because it is the new future of a new form joined in unity and relationship, the only guarantees that are known to us is that it will be a future of love, a future without fear, a future with unlimited freedom. For what more could we ask? And what more could be asked of us? (T4:12.34,35)

There is no one answer for what the New is. The New is everything that arises from pure creation, from the joining of our will with God's, from the exploration and discovery of who we truly are through the dance of unity and relationship. The end of separation is not the end of Creation—not the end of movement or expression, not the end of relating to all that is in wonder and joy, and certainly not the end of recreating the power and glory of God's love in countless interactions of all to all, and each to each.

The New is all that we would give to one another through the expression of our mutual desire to rejoice in the knowledge of what is so.

26. ACOL seems to celebrate us as being "The Accomplished," with the ego now gone. Sounds too good to be true!

MICHAEL:

To the ego, it is!

Even the formulation of this question suggests the ego once "was" and only "now" is gone, but this is not in keeping with what ACIM has taught us. The ego never truly was; it only seemed to be, and it seemed to be to the extent we believed in what we taught ourselves following the choice for separation.

We've always been the Accomplished, in the sense that we were complete in the instant God created us. We were never incomplete, and never truly lacking—we but lacked access to all that was given because we chose to experience existence without it. What has existed is our individual and collective belief that we could truly be separate from God, and we have been experiencing the ramifications of that choice for quite some time.

The reason Jesus turns to the practice of acceptance in ACOL is that once we have learned what can be learned, our continued efforts at self-improvement are tilting at windmills. There was a time when it was necessary to speak directly to the split mind, and to use contrast and other learning devices to enable the mind to learn that its precepts were simply mistaken. But once this process is complete, and there is nothing more to be learned, then our continued efforts to learn more and more with the goal undoing the ego are simply a delay. In this scenario we are like caged animals for whom the door has been thrown open, but are as yet unwilling to leave the confines of our cages.

Neither ACIM nor ACOL are Courses in modest improvement. They are Courses in complete healing, which is the full recovery of all that God has given us and held safe from all our misperceptions and false thinking. Without acceptance, this inheritance is unclaimed.

We are called in ACOL to embrace the fact that we are, and always have been, the Accomplished. What else would there be to celebrate, but our return to the safety and eternal comfort of who we truly are?

SUSAN:

Having the ego gone sounds too good to be true. ACOL abolishes the ego, and restores our true identities. It does this through "wholeheartedness." (See number 17.) Joining mind and heart, allowing the heart to lead, restores our true identities and reveals the ego's falsehood.

A mind and heart joined in union abolishes the ego. The ego-mind was what was once in charge of all your thoughts. Since the ego is incapable of learning the ego-mind had to be circumvented in order for true learning to take place. This is what A Course of Love accomplished. This learning was accomplished in you, making you The

Accomplished. As The Accomplished, you are now able to access universal mind. (T1:1.9)

We possess everything we need to live in the world. Life was never meant to include struggle, effort, and lack. It was our belief in the ego and its thought system that created a difficult world and life.

By saying you are not only accomplished, but The Accomplished, it is being said that you are already what you have sought to be. Thus, in order to live by the truth, you must live in the world as The Accomplished and cease struggling to be other than who you are in truth. (T3:16.8)

With the ego abolished, mindfulness keeps the thought system of truth first in our minds and hearts so we can live as The Accomplished.

We do not resist patterns of the ego thought patterns that may remain as echoes in our experience. We simply strive to remain aware of our hearts and minds joined in wholeheartedness. Life as The Accomplished is ceasing to adhere to rules of time we believed governed our days and years on earth. Time is a measure of learning and ACOL ends the pattern of learning.

Only you can be accomplished and your accomplishment is already complete... Accomplishment is not an end point but a given. It is not an outcome but a certainty. It says I am rather than I will be. I will be is a statement that presumes a future in which you will be someone other than who you are in the present. Unity exists only in the here and now of the present. There is no will be in unity. There is only what is. (T2:6.4,6, emphasis in original)

We exist fully accomplished within the Christ, even as we grow and change. An oak tree exists fully accomplished within the tiny acorn that represents its potential in the state of unity. Creation continues in unity. We exist outside the pattern of time, just as the oak. Our recognition of this makes us The Accomplished.

27. ACOL repeatedly says that "giving and receiving are one." Please explain.

MICHAEL:

This idea is related to the ideas concerning sacrifice that were begun in ACIM. Consider the following: *When you associate giving with sacrifice, you give only because you believe that you are somehow getting something better, and can therefore do without the thing you give.* (T-4.II.6.4) To understand that giving and receiving are one is to transcend not only the ego's view of separateness, and the accompanying level confusion, but to express this understanding through the creative extension of being.

ACIM says: *Spirit knows that the awareness of all its brothers is included in its own, as it is included in God. The power of the whole Sonship and of its Creator is therefore spirit's own fullness, rendering its creations equally whole and equal in perfection. The ego cannot prevail against a totality that includes God, and any totality must include God. Everything He created is given all His power, because it is part of Him and shares His Being with Him. Creating is the opposite of loss, as blessing is the opposite of sacrifice. Being must be extended. That is how it retains the knowledge of itself. Spirit yearns to share its being as its Creator did. Created by sharing, its will is to create. It does not wish to contain God, but wills to extend His Being.* (T-7.IX.2, emphasis added)

In this paragraph quoted above, emphasis has been added to particular ideas in ACIM that are amplified in ACOL by the concept that giving and receiving are one. First, giving and receiving are one means that there is no true "other." For giving and receiving to be one, separateness must end as a fundamental idea of what is so, and indeed, in the first underlined statement above we find emphasis in ACIM on the idea of our fundamental unity. Who do we give to, if not our Self? ACOL notes that the identity of Christ is an identity we share, and so it is truly the case that when we give, we receive.

There is a level at which this sounds like a platitude, until we realize what is emphasized later in the above quotation: it is only through the extension of being that we retain the knowledge of our Self. Thus, giving never entails a loss, for true giving engenders the most glorious gain possible, the recognition of who we truly are. Giving and receiving are a unified action, the singular vehicle of Creation by which we come into being and know ourselves as One.

ACOL echoes this when it says, *The ego is that part of yourself that clings to the idea of separation, and thus cannot grasp the basic truth of your existence: that giving and receiving are one in truth. Put another way, all this says is that in order to be your Self, you have to share your Self. What you keep you lose. This is the principle of giving and receiving that, being finally and totally understood, will free you to be wholehearted.* (C:31.14 emphasis added)

A final idea that is important to note is that it can be instinctual to place emphasis on giving, but receiving, too, is a gift to all Creation. When we receive the gifts God has prepared for us, we receive them on behalf of all Creation. As ACOL says, we create unity and relationship through unity and relationship!

28. Our "separation" from God is the source of our problem. Yet ACOL says we are "differentiated," and that this is necessary. What is the difference between being separate and being differentiated?

LAUREL:

This is a fundamental question that can be confusing. We think, "How can there be only one when I am having my own private, unique experience? Doesn't that indicate that I am separate from others, even if we come from the same source?"

In the "Forty Days and Forty Nights" of ACOL, the relationship with our differentiated experience is explained through a discussion of attributes. God is without attributes. The source can't have attributes because it is the source of everything; therefore, all is included, with no exclusions. In this way, God is All (including everything), and Nothing (without attributes of its own.)

Because this One attributeless source is continuously creating, expressing, and expanding, it has the ability to take attributes on and off in order to experience itself in different ways. This is differentiation. Through the process of differentiation, choices are made. When a choice for red is made, by default, all other colors are not chosen. In this way, the attributeless energy of love/God experiences as an attribute-full, differentiated expression of itself, unique from all other expressions. The differentiated set of attributes becomes a unique filter through which love sees itself. It is not separate from other versions of itself, but each filter creates a unique and differentiated experience.

The elevated Self of form, of which ACOL frequently speaks, happens when the differentiated experience and recognition of unity are joined. This is the second coming of Christ, referred to in both Courses. Differentiation is a far cry from a mistake, though it can be mistakenly perceived. It is love/God expressing and expanding. It is creation itself.

Michael:

Separation has nothing to do with the quantity and type of forms that perpetually and endlessly intertwine and transform within the fields of creation. Separation is a stance of the mind—a fundamental choice to be independent from God. A "god" of one's own, if you will.

Differentiation, as described above, is not a mental choice for separation, but the expression of Oneness in a multitude of particular forms. Putting on my pants in the morning does not make me separate from God; nor does changing them in the evening before meeting friends for dinner.

I can dress up in as many different costumes as I like, but none of this need change my identity. When we discover, as described so well above, that we are able to sustain the awareness of unity while we wear different costumes, then we have freed ourselves of *body identification*, and we are able to express who we truly are in any costume.

To suggest that the costume itself is the error, is to make once again the fundamental error of confusing the mind with the body. It is a very subtle form of *body identification* that hinges on the erroneous belief that a costume would have the power to change who we truly are.

29. ACOL speaks of the fulfillment of the Way of Jesus, and then introduces the Way of Mary. What does this mean?

MICHAEL:

This is, for me, a beautiful section of ACOL that ties in to the essential theme of transcending the time of learning, and moving into the time of creation. ACOL notes that not only Jesus but his mother Mary *realized full Christ-consciousness and full expression of Christ-consciousness in form.* (D:Day17.9)

Jesus' life is described as "the example life," the focus of which was upon teaching by example, and preparing the way for others who also would come to accept their true identity, and lead example lives of teaching and learning. Mary, on the other hand, demonstrated the way of creation, and prepared the way for those who would approach Christ-consciousness through relationship. At the present time both Ways work together to bring about the fulfillment of the time of Christ, which is related to the end of learning and the beginning of the New.

What Jesus represented or demonstrated has now been realized, which is why this is called the time of Christ. The "time" of Christ, whom so many associate with Jesus Christ, represents the "time" of fulfillment of the way of Jesus. What could be taught and learned has been taught and learned. Now it is time to move beyond what could be taught and learned to what can only be realized through relationship. Now is the time of the final revelation of what can be realized, or made real, through following the example life of Jesus. (D:Day17.12)

In ACOL, the Way of Jesus and the Way of Mary are both described as necessary at this time, for they work hand-in-hand, but the ways are not identical. According to ACOL, *One way is active. One way is receptive. Yet the ways are not separate any more than Jesus was separate from Mary—or any mother separate from her child. The ways are rather complimentary and symbiotic. Together they return wholeness and will bring about the completion of the time of Christ.* (D:Day18.2) ACOL also says, *Mary represents the relationship that occurs within, Jesus the relationship that occurs with the world.* (D:Day18.2) The Way of Mary is about receiving, while the Way of Jesus is about action.

Regardless of the "ways" to which we feel called—to one, or the other, or both—ACOL suggests that what is essential at this time is making our feelings known, or visible, as *they are the creations unique to you through your interaction with the Christ-consciousness that abides in you.* (D:Day18.11) The fulfillment of the time of Christ, and our creation of the New through unity and relationship will come through the various ways in which each of us "make known" the reality of Christ within us.

As ACOL says, *All are called to become, but some must "do" in order to "become." Those called to the way of Mary are not required to do in the sense of fulfilling a specific function that will become manifest in the world, but are required to do in the sense of receiving, sharing, and being what they are asked to become. This is an act of incarnation, and is a new pattern, a pattern of what can be imagined being made real, not through doing, but through the creative act of incarnating in union with spirit. It corresponds with the end of the way of Jesus in that the way of incarnation is the way of miracles. It corresponds with the end of the way of Jesus in that an example is provided. It differs only in that the example is not an example of an individuated life but an example of the union and relationship that is all life.* (D:Day19.10)

The Way of Mary is a new pattern, related not to teaching and learning, but to making the Christ within us known by birthing the very truth of who we are. The Way of Mary is about direct incarnation, and receptivity, and does not require worldly action as a vehicle for transformation. What can be imagined is made real through us. ACOL suggests that eventually all will follow the Way of Mary, though for a time the Way of Jesus and the Way of Mary will continue to work together to bring about the fulfillment of the time of Christ.

30. I have heard that ACOL concludes with a "Forty Days and Forty Nights" section in the final book. Can you summarize the content of that section?

LAUREL:

The "Forty Days and Nights" of ACOL is a virtual trip to the mountaintop with Jesus as guide. This trip to the mountaintop doesn't remove you from normal life; it actually uses your own life experiences as curriculum.

The previous teachings of ACOL culminate here, offering a uniquely personal journey of exploration and revelation during which you are guided to apply the principles to your own experiences. Students who open themselves to hands-on discovery while working with The Forty report enjoying happier, freer lives with a deeper knowing of the unity of all things. The Forty offers a beautiful and intimate treasure that leads to lasting transformation.

Resources

FOR FURTHER INFORMATION ABOUT ACOL, PLEASE CONSIDER THE FOLLOWING:

Mari Perron, ACOL's First Receiver, offers "Dialogue in Motion" and "The Jesus Chronicles" at *www.mariperron.com*

Additional dialogues and expressions are offered by Mari Perron at *www.centerforacourseoflove.org*

A large selection of background information about ACOL can be found at *www.acourseoflove.org*

Numerous video and audio interviews with Mari Perron are available on all three websites mentioned above.

ACOL is available in four formats: quality softcover, gift-quality hardcover, as an ebook, and as an audiobook, available at bookstores and online

A 48-page introduction to ACOL, *A Course of Love: An Overview* by Celia Hales is available online or at *www.acourseoflove.org*

Highlights From A Course of Love, a 236-page collection of "highlights" compiled by Paula Payne Hardin is available online or at *www. acourseoflove.org*

A "search inside the text" of ACOL feature is available at *www.centerforacourseoflove.org* and *www.acourseoflove.org*. You can also "search inside the text" of both ACIM and ACOL simultaneously at either of the above websites or at *http://cocreatingclarity.org/ACIMOE-ACOL/*

Links to foreign language translations of ACOL can be found at *www.acourseoflove.org*

An "ACOL Access App" is available for your device which provides an automatic daily notification of the ACOL Quotation of the Day. A link to the app, as well as the Quotation of the Day is available on the homepage of *www.acourseoflove.org*.

Twenty-four chapters from ACOL and eight audiobook chapters are available for free. See the homepage of *www.acourseoflove.org*

A free monthly newsletter, "The Embrace," features articles written by those inspired by ACOL. See the hompage of *www.acourseoflove.org* to subscribe.

For those who wish to integrate ACOL more deeply into daily life, it if often helpful to participate in a "sharing" group. Many such groups, both in-person and online, are available. See *www.acourseoflove.org* under the "Groups" tab for listings.

Made in the USA
Middletown, DE
23 February 2021